Contents

Preface

Welcome to *Computer Concepts—Illustrated Essentials, Third Edition.* If this is your first experience with the Illustrated series, you'll see that this book has a unique design: each concept is presented on two facing pages, with text and definitions on the left and illustrations on the right. The layout makes it easy to focus on a single topic without having to read a lot of text and flip pages to find an illustration.

This book is an ideal learning tool for a wide range of learners—the "rookies" will find the clean design easy to follow and focused with only essential information presented, and the "hotshots" will appreciate being able to move quickly through the lessons to find the information they need without reading a lot of text. The design also makes this a great reference after the course is over! See the illustration on the right to learn more about the pedagogical and design elements of a typical lesson.

About This Edition

- **Coverage**—Covers essential computer concepts such as computer system basics, input and output devices, memory, storage, networks, security, and software.

- **Fully Updated.** Updated examples highlight new technologies including Slate computers, converging technologies, Windows 7 and cloud computing.

- **Ideal Supplement**—Works well as a supplement to other text materials to enhance any course.

Each two-page spread focuses on a single concept.

Introduction briefly explains why the lesson concept is important.

A case scenario puts the lesson concept in context.

Understanding Storage Media

RAM retains data only while the power is on, so your computer must have a more permanent storage option. As Figure A-9 shows, a storage device receives data from RAM and stores it on a storage medium, some of which are described below. Later the data can be read and sent back to RAM to use again. All data and programs are stored as files. A computer **file** is a named collection of stored data. An **executable file** contains the instructions that tell a computer how to perform a specific task; for instance, the files that are used while the computer starts are executable. A **data file** is created by a user, usually with software. For instance, a report that you write with a word processing program is data, and must be saved as a data file if you want to access it later. Kevin explains the types of storage media available.

DETAILS

The types of storage media are discussed below:

- **Magnetic storage media** store data as magnetized particles on a surface. A **hard disk**, also called a hard disk drive, is the most common type of magnetic storage media. It contains several magnetic oxide-covered metal platters that are usually sealed in a case inside the computer. You can also purchase external hard drives for extra or backup storage.

QUICK TIP
Optical storage devices, such as CDs and DVDs, are much more durable than magnetic storage media.

- **Optical storage devices** are polycarbonate discs coated with a reflective metal on which data is stored using laser technology as a trail of tiny pits or dark spots in the surface of the disc. The data that these pits or spots represent can then be "read" with a beam of laser light.
  - The first standard optical storage device available for personal computers was the **CD (compact disc)**. One CD can store 700 MB of data.
  - A **DVD**, though the same size as a CD, can store between 4.7 and 15.9 GB of data, depending on whether data is stored on one or two sides of the disc, and how many layers of data each side contains. The term DVD is no longer an acronym, although it was originally an acronym for *digital video disc* and later was sometimes updated to *digital versatile disc.*
  - **Blu-ray** discs store 25 GB of data per layer. They are used for storing high-definition video.
- **Flash memory** (also called **solid state storage**) is similar to ROM except that it can be written to more than once. **Flash memory cards** are small, portable cards encased in hard plastic to which data can be written and rewritten. They are used in digital cameras, handheld computers, video game controllers, and other devices.
- A popular type of flash memory is a **USB flash storage device**, also called a **USB drive** or a **flash drive**. See Figure A-10.

QUICK TIP
There is only one way to insert a flash drive, so if you're having problems inserting the drive into the slot, turn the drive over and try again.

  - USB drives for personal computers are available in a wide range of sizes from one to 64 GB of data. They are becoming more popular for use as a secondary or backup storage device for data typically stored on a hard disk drive.
  - USB drives plug directly into the USB port of a personal computer; the computer recognizes the device as another disk drive. The location and letter designation of USB ports varies with the brand and model of computer you are using, but the physical port may be on the front, back, or side of a computer.
  - USB flash storage devices are about the size of a pack of gum and often have a ring that you can attach to a key chain.

Concepts 10   Understanding Essential Computer Concepts

Tips and troubleshooting advice, provide helpful information related to the lesson text.

iv

Computer Concepts

ILLUSTRATED - Third Edition

Essentials

Katherine T. Pinard

COURSE TECHNOLOGY
CENGAGE Learning

Australia • Brazil • Japan • Korea • Mexico • Singapore • Spain • United Kingdom • United States

COURSE TECHNOLOGY
CENGAGE Learning™

**Computer Concepts—Illustrated Essentials,
Third Edition**

Katherine T. Pinard

Vice President, Publisher: Nicole Jones Pinard

Executive Editor: Marjorie Hunt

Associate Acquisitions Editor: Brandi Shailer

Senior Product Manager: Christina Kling Garrett

Associate Product Manager: Michelle Camisa

Editorial Assistant: Kim Klasner

Director of Marketing: Cheryl Costantini

Senior Marketing Manager: Ryan DeGrote

Marketing Coordinator: Kristen Panciocco

Developmental Editor: Kim Crowley

Content Project Manager: Heather Hopkins

Copy Editor: John Bosco

Proofreader: Harold Johnson

Indexer: BIM Indexing and Proofreading Services

QA Manuscript Reviewer: Jeff Schwartz

Print Buyer: Fola Orekoya

Cover Designer: GEX Publishing Services

Cover Artist: Mark Hunt

Composition: GEX Publishing Services

For product information and technology assistance, contact us at
Cengage Learning Customer & Sales Support, 1-800-354-9706
For permission to use material from this text or product, submit all requests online at **www.cengage.com/permissions**
Further permissions questions can be emailed to
permissionrequest@cengage.com

Library of Congress Control Number: 2010931917

ISBN-13: 978-0-538-75390-6
ISBN-10: 0-538-75390-0

Course Technology
20 Channel Center Street
Boston, MA 02210
USA

Cengage Learning is a leading provider of customized learning solutions with office locations around the globe, including Singapore, the United Kingdom, Australia, Mexico, Brazil, and Japan. Locate your local office at:
international.cengage.com/region

Cengage Learning products are represented in Canada by Nelson Education, Ltd.

To learn more about Course Technology, visit **www.cengage.com/coursetechnology**

To learn more about Cengage Learning, visit **www.cengage.com**

Purchase any of our products at your local college store or at our preferred online store **www.cengagebrain.com**

Printed in the United States of America
1 2 3 4 5 6 7 8 9 18 17 16 15 14 13 12 11 10

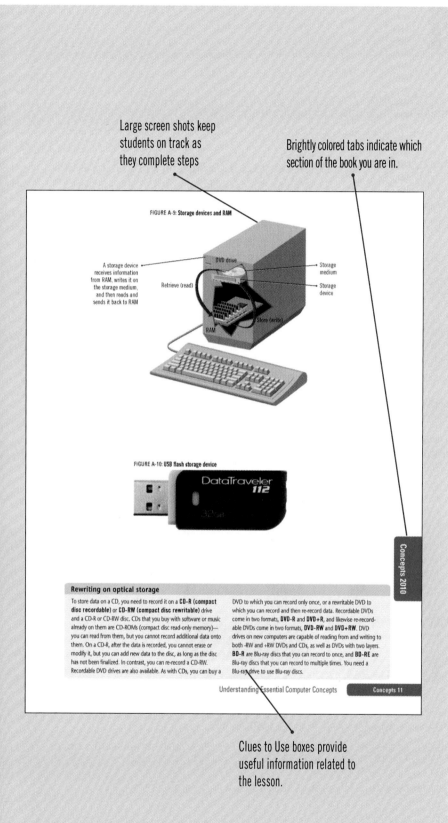

Large screen shots keep students on track as they complete steps

Brightly colored tabs indicate which section of the book you are in.

FIGURE A-9: Storage devices and RAM

A storage device receives information from RAM, writes it on the storage medium, and then reads and sends it back to RAM

DVD drive

Retrieve (read)

Storage medium

Storage device

Store (write)

RAM

FIGURE A-10: USB flash storage device

DataTraveler 112

Rewriting on optical storage

To store data on a CD, you need to record it on a **CD-R (compact disc recordable)** or **CD-RW (compact disc rewritable)** drive and a CD-R or CD-RW disc. CDs that you buy with software or music already on them are CD-ROMs (compact disc read-only memory)—you can read from them, but you cannot record additional data onto them. On a CD-R, after the data is recorded, you cannot erase or modify it, but you can add new data to the disc, as long as the disc has not been finalized. In contrast, you can re-record a CD-RW. Recordable DVD drives are also available. As with CDs, you can buy a

DVD to which you can record only once, or a rewritable DVD to which you can record and then re-record data. Recordable DVDs come in two formats, **DVD-R** and **DVD+R**, and likewise re-recordable DVDs come in two formats, **DVD-RW** and **DVD+RW**. DVD drives on new computers are capable of reading from and writing to both -RW and +RW DVDs and CDs, as well as DVDs with two layers. **BD-R** are Blu-ray discs that you can record to once, and **BD-RE** are Blu-ray discs that you can record to multiple times. You need a Blu-ray drive to use Blu-ray discs.

Understanding Essential Computer Concepts

Concepts 11

Clues to Use boxes provide useful information related to the lesson.

Assignments

The lessons use Quest Specialty Travel, a fictional adventure travel company, as the case study. The assignments on the light yellow pages at the end of each unit increase in difficulty. Assignments include:

- **Concepts Review** consist of multiple choice, matching, and screen identification questions.

- **Skills Reviews** are hands-on, step-by-step exercises that review the skills covered in each lesson in the unit.

- **Independent Challenges** are case projects requiring critical thinking and understanding of the unit concepts. The Independent Challenges increase in difficulty, with the first one in each unit being the easiest. Independent Challenges 2 and 3 become increasingly open-ended, requiring more independent problem solving.

- **Real Life Independent Challenge** is a practical exercise in which students follow steps to purchase their own computer system and software, including researching and organizing information comparing prices, and working within a budget.

- **Advanced Challenge Exercises** set within the Independent Challenges provide optional steps for more advanced students.

About SAM

SAM is the premier proficiency-based assessment and training environment for Microsoft Office. Web-based software along with an inviting user interface provide maximum teaching and learning flexibility. SAM builds students' skills and confidence with a variety of real-life simulations, and SAM Projects' assignments prepare students for today's workplace.

The SAM system includes Assessment, Training, and Projects, featuring page references and remediation for this book as well as Course Technology's Microsoft Office textbooks. With SAM, instructors can enjoy the flexibility of creating assignments based on content from their favorite Microsoft Office books or based on specific course objectives. Instructors appreciate the scheduling and reporting options that have made SAM the market-leading online testing and training software for over a decade. Over 2,000 performance-based questions and matching Training simulations, as well as tens of thousands of objective-based questions from many Course Technology texts, provide instructors with a variety of choices across multiple applications from the introductory level through the comprehensive level. The inclusion of hands-on Projects guarantee that student knowledge will skyrocket from the practice of solving real-world situations using Microsoft Office software.

SAM Assessment

- Content for these hands-on, performance-based tasks includes Word, Excel, Access, PowerPoint, Internet Explorer, Outlook, and Windows. Includes tens of thousands of objective-based questions from many Course Technology texts.

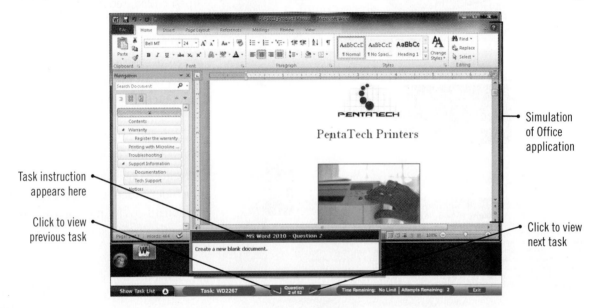

Task instruction appears here

Click to view previous task

Simulation of Office application

Click to view next task

SAM Training

- Observe mode allows the student to watch and listen to a task as it is being completed.
- Practice mode allows the student to follow guided arrows and hear audio prompts to help visual learners know how to complete a task.
- Apply mode allows the student to prove what they've learned by completing a task using helpful instructions.

SAM Projects

- Live-in-the-application assignments in Word, Excel, Access and PowerPoint that help students be sure they know how to effectively communicate, solve a problem or make a decision.
- Students receive detailed feedback on their project within minutes.
- Additionally, teaches proper file management techniques.
- Ensures that academic integrity is not compromised, with unique anti-cheating detection encrypted into the data files.

Instructor Resources

The Instructor Resources CD is Course Technology's way of putting the resources and information needed to teach and learn effectively into your hands. With an integrated array of teaching and learning tools that offer you and your students a broad range of technology-based instructional options, we believe this CD represents the highest quality and most cutting edge resources available to instructors today. The resources available with this book are:

- **Instructor's Manual**—Available as an electronic file, the Instructor's Manual includes detailed lecture topics with teaching tips for each unit.

- **Sample Syllabus**—Prepare and customize your course easily using this sample course outline.

- **PowerPoint Presentations**—Each unit has a corresponding PowerPoint presentation that you can use in lecture, distribute to your students, or customize to suit your course.

- **Figure Files**—The figures in the text are provided on the Instructor Resources CD to help you illustrate key topics or concepts. You can create traditional overhead transparencies by printing the figure files. Or you can create electronic slide shows by using the figures in a presentation program such as PowerPoint.

- **Solutions to Exercises**—Solutions to Exercises contains every file students are asked to create or modify in the lessons and end-of-unit material. Also provided in this section, there is a document outlining the solutions for the end-of-unit Concepts Review, Skills Review, and Independent Challenges. An Annotated Solution File and Grading Rubric accompany each file and can be used together for quick and easy grading.

- **ExamView**—ExamView is a powerful testing software package that allows you to create and administer printed, computer (LAN-based), and Internet exams. ExamView includes hundreds of questions that correspond to the topics covered in this text, enabling students to generate detailed study guides that include page references for further review. The computer-based and Internet testing components allow students to take exams at their computers, and also saves you time by grading each exam automatically.

Content for Online Learning.

Course Technology has partnered with the leading distance learning solution providers and class-management platforms today. To access this material, visit www.cengage.com/webtutor and search for your title. Instructor resources include the following: additional case projects, sample syllabi, PowerPoint presentations, and more. For additional information, please contact your sales representative. For students to access this material, they must have purchased a WebTutor PIN-code specific to this title and your campus platform. The resources for students might include (based on instructor preferences): topic reviews, review questions, practice tests, and more.

COURSECASTS Learning on the Go. Always Available...Always Relevant.

Our fast-paced world is driven by technology. You know because you are an active participant—always on the go, always keeping up with technological trends, and always learning new ways to embrace technology to power your life. Let CourseCasts, hosted by Ken Baldauf of Florida State University, be your guide into weekly updates in this ever-changing space. These timely, relevant podcasts are produced weekly and are available for download at http://coursecasts.course.com or directly from iTunes (search by CourseCasts). CourseCasts are a perfect solution to getting students (and even instructors) to learn on the go!

Credits

Figures 1, 14 & 25: © iStockphoto.com

Figure 2: PRNewsFoto/Verizon Wireless

Figure 3: Courtesy of NASA

Figure 4: Courtesy of Intel Corporation

Figure 5: Courtesy of AMD

Figure 10: Courtesy of Kingston Digital Inc.

Figures 11a & 12b: Courtesy of Logitech

Figures 11b, 12a & 21-24: Courtesy of © 2010 Microsoft Corporation. All rights reserved. Microsoft product screenshot(s) reprinted with permission from Microsoft Corporation

Figures 13a & 13b: Courtesy of IBM Corporation

Figures 15a, 15b, & 16: Courtesy of Hewlett-Packard Company

Figure 17: Courtesy of Belkin

Figure 18: Courtesy of D-Link Systems, Inc.

Figure 20: Courtesy of Trend Micro Inc.

Acknowledgements

Author Acknowledgements

Thank you to Kim, my developmental editor, who as usual, made even this tiny book better with her edits.

– Katherine T. Pinard

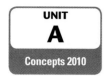

Understanding Essential Computer Concepts

Computers are essential tools in almost all kinds of activity in virtually every type of business. In this unit, you will learn about computers and their components. You will learn about input and output, how a computer processes data and stores information, how information is transmitted, and ways to secure that information. ▄▄▄▄ Quest Specialty Travel is expanding its North American offices and just purchased Sheehan Tours, an established travel agency in Boston, Massachusetts. Sheehan Tours has been in business for over 40 years and has a large customer base. Unfortunately, its computer system is outdated. Its office contains a hodge-podge of computer equipment, most of which was purchased used, and only one computer is connected to the Internet. Kevin O'Brien, the manager of the New York office, has been sent to the new Boston office to help them switch to Quest's business practices. He has already ordered and installed new computer equipment. His next task is to teach the staff how to use the new equipment.

OBJECTIVES

Investigate types of computers

Examine computer systems

Investigate data representation

Understand memory

Understand storage media

Examine input devices

Examine output devices

Explore data communications

Learn about networks

Learn about security threats

Understand system software

Understand application software

Investigating Types of Computers

A **computer** is an electronic device that accepts information and instructions from a user, manipulates the information according to the instructions, displays the information in some way, and stores the information for retrieval later. Computers are classified by their size, speed, and capabilities.  Most of the staff at Sheehan Tours do not know anything about computers except for the ones that sit on their desks, so Kevin decides to start with a basic explanation of the types of computers available.

DETAILS

The following list describes various types of computers:

- **Personal computers (PCs)** are computers typically used by a single user, for use in the home or office. Personal computers are used for general computing tasks such as word processing, manipulating numbers, working with photographs or graphics, exchanging email, and accessing the Internet. In common usage, the term "PC" refers to personal computers that use Microsoft Windows. Personal computers that are sold only by Apple, Inc. are referred to as Macs (short for Macintosh).

- The following are types of personal computers:

  - **Desktop computers** are designed to sit compactly on a desk.
  - **Notebook computers** (also referred to as **laptop computers**), similar to the one shown in Figure A-1, are small, lightweight, and designed for portability.
  - **Tablet PCs** are notebook computers that have a screen on which the user can write with a stylus.
  - **Subnotebook computers**, sometimes called **ultraportable computers** or **mini notebooks** are notebook computers that are smaller and lighter than ordinary notebooks. **Netbooks**, a type of sub-notebook computers, are notebooks that are primarily designed to allow users to access the Internet and check email.
  - **Slate computers** are thin computers that do not have an external keyboard or a mouse. Users touch the screen or use a stylus to accomplish tasks. Slate computers are primarily used to read electronic books, view video, and access the Internet.

- **Hand-held computers** are small computers that fit in the palm of your hand. Hand-held computers have more limited capabilities than personal computers.

  - **Smartphones**, like the one shown in Figure A-2, are used to make and receive phone calls, maintain an address book, electronic appointment book, calculator, and notepad, send email, connect to the Internet, play music, take photos or video, and even perform some of the same functions as a PC, such as word processing.
  - **MP3 players** are hand-held computers that are primarily used to store and play music, although some models can also be used to play digital movies or television shows.

- **Mainframe computers** are used by larger businesses and government agencies to provide centralized storage, processing, and management for large amounts of data. The price of a mainframe computer varies widely, from several hundred thousand dollars to close to one million dollars.

- The largest and fastest computers, called **supercomputers**, are used by large corporations and government agencies when the tremendous volume of data would seriously delay processing on a mainframe computer. A supercomputer, like the one shown in Figure A-3, can cost millions of dollars.

Converging technologies

Every year, the lines between the types of computers are growing more and more blurry. Handheld devices like smartphones are more powerful than the first notebook computers were, and today's desktop PCs are far more powerful than the mainframe computers of a few decades ago. As new technologies are developed, consumers will need fewer and fewer devices to accomplish their tasks.

FIGURE A-1: Notebook computer

FIGURE A-2: Smartphone

FIGURE A-3: Supercomputer

Understanding Essential Computer Concepts

Examining Computer Systems

A **computer system** includes computer hardware and software. **Hardware** refers to the physical components of a computer. **Software** refers to the intangible components of a computer system, particularly the **programs**, or lists of instructions, that the computer needs to perform a specific task. The **operating system** is special software that controls basic input and output, allocates system resources, manages storage space, maintains security, and detects equipment failure.  Kevin explains how computers work and points out the main components of a computer system.

DETAILS

The following list provides an overview of computer system components and how they work:

- The design and construction of a computer is referred to as its **architecture** or **configuration**. The technical details about each hardware component are called **specifications**. For example, a computer system might be configured to include a printer; a specification for that printer might be a print speed of eight pages per minute or the capacity to print in color.

- The hardware and the software of a computer system work together to process data. **Data** refers to the words, numbers, figures, sounds, and graphics that describe people, events, things, and ideas. Modifying data is referred to as **processing**.

- In a computer, processing tasks occur on the **motherboard**, which is located inside the computer and is the main electronic component of the computer. See Figure A-4. The motherboard is a **circuit board**, which is a rigid piece of insulating material with **circuits**—electrical paths—on it that control specific functions. The motherboard contains the following processing hardware:

  - The **microprocessor**, also called the **processor** or the **central processing unit (CPU)**, consists of transistors and electronic circuits on a silicon chip (an integrated circuit embedded in semiconductor material). See Figure A-5. The processor is mounted on the motherboard and is responsible for executing instructions to process information.

  - **Cards** are removable circuit boards that are inserted into slots in the motherboard to expand the capabilities of the motherboard. For example, a sound card translates the digital audio information from the computer into analog sounds that the human ear can hear.

- The data or instructions you type into the computer are called **input**. The result of the computer processing input is referred to as **output**. The computer itself takes care of the processing functions, but it needs additional components, called **peripheral devices**, to accomplish the input, output, and storage functions.

  - You use an **input device**, such as a keyboard or a mouse, to enter data and issue commands. **Commands** are input instructions that tell the computer how to process data. For example, you might want to center the title and double-space the text of a report. You use the appropriate commands in the word processing program that instruct the computer to modify the data you have input so the report text is double-spaced and the report title is centered.

  - Output can be in many different forms, including reports, documents, graphs, sounds, and pictures. Computers produce output using **output devices**, such as a monitor or printer.

  - The output you create using a computer can be stored either inside the computer itself or on an external storage device, such as a DVD. You will learn more about storage devices later in this unit.

FIGURE A-4: Motherboard

FIGURE A-5: Microprocessor (front and back views)

Comparing microprocessor speeds

How fast a computer can process instructions depends partially on the speed of the microprocessor. Among other factors, the speed of the microprocessor is determined by its clock speed, word size, and whether it is single or dual core. **Clock speed** is measured in **megahertz (MHz)**, millions of cycles per second, or in **gigahertz (GHz)**, billions of cycles per second. **Word size** refers to the number of bits—the smallest unit of information in a computer—that are processed at one time; for example, a 32-bit processor processes 32 bits at a time. A computer with a large word size can process faster than a computer with a small word size. PCs come with 32-bit or 64-bit processors. Finally, a **dual-core processor**, one that has two processors on a single chip, can process information up to twice as fast as a **single-core processor**, one with one processor on the chip. Likewise, a **quad-core processor**, with four processors on a chip, processes information up to four times as fast as a single-core processor.

Investigating Data Representation

In order to understand how data is processed in a computer, you first need to learn how the computer represents and stores data. To a computer, the characters used in human language, such as the characters in a word processed document, are meaningless because it is an electronic device. Kevin gives a basic description of how information is represented inside a computer.

The following information will help you understand data processing:

- Like a light bulb, the computer must interpret every signal as either "on" or "off." To do this, a computer represents data as distinct or separate numbers. Specifically, it represents "on" with a 1 and "off" with a 0. These numbers are referred to as **binary digits**, or **bits**.

- A series of eight bits is called a **byte**. As Figure A-6 shows, the byte that represents the integer value 0 is 00000000, with all eight bits "off" or set to 0. The byte that represents the integer value 1 is 00000001, and the byte that represents 255 is 11111111.

- A **kilobyte (KB** or simply **K)** is 1024 bytes, or approximately one thousand bytes. A **megabyte (MB)** is 1,048,576 bytes, or about one million bytes. A **gigabyte (GB)** is 1,073,741,824 bytes, or about one billion bytes. A **terabyte (TB)** is 1,024 GB, or approximately one trillion bytes.

- Personal computers commonly use the ASCII system to represent character data. **ASCII** (pronounced "ASK-ee") stands for **American Standard Code for Information Interchange**. Each ASCII number represents an English character. Computers translate ASCII into binary data so that they can process it.

  - The original ASCII system used 7 bits to represent the numbers 0 (0000000) through 127 (1111111) to stand for 128 common characters and nonprinting control characters. Because bits are usually arranged in bytes, the eighth bit is reserved for error checking.

  - Extended ASCII uses eight bits and includes the numbers 128 (10000000) through 255 (11111111) to represent additional characters and symbols. Extended ASCII was developed to add codes for punctuation marks, symbols, such as $ and ©, and additional characters, such as é and ü, that were not included in the original 128 codes.

  - Most computers use the original ASCII definitions, but not all computers use the same definitions for Extended ASCII. Computers that run the Windows operating system use the set of Extended ASCII definitions defined by the American National Standards Institute (ANSI). Figure A-7 shows sample ASCII code with ANSI standard Extended ASCII characters.

FIGURE A-6: Binary representation of numbers

Number	Binary representation
0	00000000
1	00000001
2	00000010
3	00000011
4	00000100
5	00000101
6	00000110
7	00000111
8	00001000
⋮	⋮
253	11111101
254	11111110
255	11111111

FIGURE A-7: Sample ASCII code representing letters and symbols

Character	ASCII Code	Binary Number
(space)	32	00100000
$	36	00100100
A	65	01000001
B	66	01000010
a	97	01100001
b	98	01100010
?	129	10000001
£	163	10100011
®	217	11011001
é	233	11101001

Understanding Memory

In addition to the microprocessor, another important component of personal computer hardware is the **memory**, which stores instructions and data. Your computer has five types of memory: random access memory, cache memory, virtual memory, read-only memory, and complementary metal oxide semiconductor memory. Kevin realizes that most of the Sheehan Tours staff don't understand the difference between memory types, so he explains the different types of memory.

DETAILS

Types of memory include the following:

QUICK TIP

When the computer is off, RAM is empty.

- **Random access memory (RAM)** temporarily holds programs and data while the computer is on and allows the computer to access that information randomly; in other words, RAM doesn't need to access data in the same sequence in which it was stored. For example, if you are writing a report, the microprocessor temporarily copies the word processing program you are using into RAM so the microprocessor can quickly access the instructions that you will need as you type and format your report. The characters you type are also stored in RAM, along with the character formats, graphics, and other objects that you might use. RAM consists of chips on cards that plug into the motherboard.

  - Most personal computers use **synchronous dynamic random access memory (SDRAM)**, which is synchronized with the processor to allow faster access to its contents.
  - RAM is sometimes referred to as **volatile memory** or **temporary memory** because it is constantly changing as long as the computer is on and is cleared when the computer is turned off.
  - **Memory capacity**, sometimes referred to as **storage capacity**, is the amount of data that the computer can handle at any given time and is measured in megabytes or gigabytes. For example, a computer that has 2 GB of RAM has the capacity to temporarily store more than two billion bits of data at one time.

- **Cache memory**, sometimes called **RAM cache** or **CPU cache**, is a special, high-speed memory chip on the motherboard or CPU itself that stores frequently accessed and recently accessed data and commands instead of in RAM.

QUICK TIP

You can often add more RAM to a computer by installing additional memory cards on the motherboard. You cannot add ROM; it is permanently installed on the motherboard.

- **Virtual memory** is space on the computer's storage devices that simulates additional RAM. It enables programs to run as if your computer had more RAM by moving data and commands from RAM to the computer's permanent storage device and swapping in the new data and commands. See Figure A-8. Virtual memory, however, is much slower than RAM.

- **Read-only memory (ROM)** is a chip on the motherboard that has been prerecorded with data. ROM permanently stores the set of instructions that the computer uses to check the computer system's components to make sure they are working and to activate the essential software that controls the processing function when you turn the computer on.

QUICK TIP

The act of turning on the computer is sometimes called **booting up**.

  - ROM contains a set of instructions called the **BIOS (basic input/output system)**, which tells the computer to initialize the motherboard, how to recognize devices connected to the computer, and to start the boot process. The **boot process** is the set of events that occurs between the moment you turn on the computer and the moment you can begin to use the computer. The set of instructions for executing the boot process is stored in ROM.
  - ROM never changes and it remains intact when the computer is turned off; therefore, it is called **nonvolatile memory** or **permanent memory**.

- **Complementary metal oxide semiconductor (CMOS**, pronounced "SEE-moss") **memory** is a chip installed on the motherboard that is activated during the boot process and identifies where essential software is stored.

  - A small rechargeable battery powers CMOS so its contents are saved when the computer is turned off. CMOS changes every time you add or remove hardware on your computer system.
  - CMOS, often referred to as **semipermanent memory**, changes when hardware is added or removed, but doesn't empty when the computer is shut off.
  - Because CMOS retains its contents when the computer is turned off, the date and time are stored there.

FIGURE A-8: How virtual memory works

1. Your computer is running a word processing program that takes up most of the program area in RAM, but you want to run a spreadsheet program at the same time.

2. The operating system moves the least-used segment of the word processing program into virtual memory on the computer's permanent storage device (hard disk drive).

3. The spreadsheet program can now be loaded into the RAM vacated by the least-used segment of the word processing program.

4. If the least-used segment of the word processing program is later needed, it is copied from virtual memory back into RAM. To make room, some other infrequently used segment of a program will need to be transferred into virtual memory.

Upgrading RAM

One of the easiest ways to make your computer run faster is to add more RAM. The more RAM a computer has, the more instructions and data can be stored there. You can often add more RAM to a computer by installing additional memory cards on the motherboard. Currently, you can buy from 512 MB to 16 GB RAM cards, and usually, you can add more than one card. Check your computer's specifications to see what size RAM cards the slots on your motherboard will accept. Note that if your computer has a 32-bit processor, it can't use more than 4 GB of RAM, even if the computer has places to plug in more cards.

Understanding Storage Media

RAM retains data only while the power is on, so your computer must have a more permanent storage option. As Figure A-9 shows, a storage device receives data from RAM and stores it on a storage medium, some of which are described below. Later the data can be read and sent back to RAM to use again. All data and programs are stored as files. A computer **file** is a named collection of stored data. An **executable file** contains the instructions that tell a computer how to perform a specific task; for instance, the files that are used while the computer starts are executable. A **data file** is created by a user, usually with software. For instance, a report that you write with a word processing program is data, and must be saved as a data file if you want to access it later. Kevin explains the types of storage media available.

DETAILS

The types of storage media are discussed below:

- **Magnetic storage media** store data as magnetized particles on a surface. A **hard disk**, also called a hard disk drive, is the most common type of magnetic storage media. It contains several magnetic oxide-covered metal platters that are usually sealed in a case inside the computer. You can also purchase external hard drives for extra or backup storage.

- **Optical storage devices** are polycarbonate discs coated with a reflective metal on which data is stored using laser technology as a trail of tiny pits or dark spots in the surface of the disc. The data that these pits or spots represent can then be "read" with a beam of laser light.

  - The first standard optical storage device available for personal computers was the **CD (compact disc)**. One CD can store 700 MB of data.
  - A **DVD**, though the same size as a CD, can store between 4.7 and 15.9 GB of data, depending on whether data is stored on one or two sides of the disc, and how many layers of data each side contains. The term *DVD* is no longer an acronym, although it was originally an acronym for *digital video disc* and later was sometimes updated to *digital versatile disc*.
  - **Blu-ray** discs store 25 GB of data per layer. They are used for storing high-definition video.

- **Flash memory** (also called **solid state storage**) is similar to ROM except that it can be written to more than once. **Flash memory cards** are small, portable cards encased in hard plastic to which data can be written and rewritten. They are used in digital cameras, handheld computers, video game controllers, and other devices.

- A popular type of flash memory is a **USB flash storage device**, also called a **USB drive** or a **flash drive**. See Figure A-10.

  - USB drives for personal computers are available in a wide range of sizes from one to 64 GB of data. They are becoming more popular for use as a secondary or backup storage device for data typically stored on a hard disk drive.
  - USB drives plug directly into the USB port of a personal computer; the computer recognizes the device as another disk drive. The location and letter designation of USB ports varies with the brand and model of computer you are using, but the physical port may be on the front, back, or side of a computer.
  - USB flash storage devices are about the size of a pack of gum and often have a ring that you can attach to a key chain.

QUICK TIP
Optical storage devices, such as CDs and DVDs, are much more durable than magnetic storage media.

QUICK TIP
There is only one way to insert a flash drive, so if you're having problems inserting the drive into the slot, turn the drive over and try again.

Understanding Essential Computer Concepts

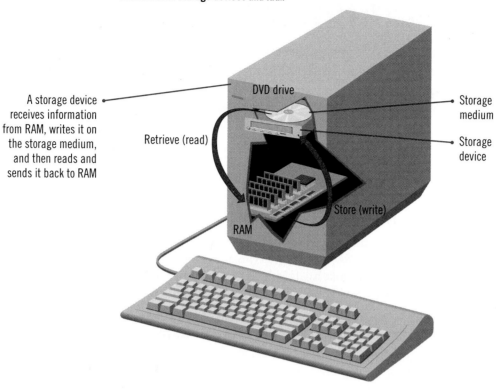

A storage device receives information from RAM, writes it on the storage medium, and then reads and sends it back to RAM

DVD drive

Retrieve (read)

Store (write)

RAM

Storage medium

Storage device

FIGURE A-10: USB flash storage device

DataTraveler 112

32GB

Concepts 2010

Rewriting on optical storage

To store data on a CD, you need to record it on a **CD-R (compact disc recordable)** or **CD-RW (compact disc rewritable)** drive and a CD-R or CD-RW disc. CDs that you buy with software or music already on them are CD-ROMs (compact disc read-only memory)—you can read from them, but you cannot record additional data onto them. On a CD-R, after the data is recorded, you cannot erase or modify it, but you can add new data to the disc, as long as the disc has not been finalized. In contrast, you can re-record a CD-RW. Recordable DVD drives are also available. As with CDs, you can buy a DVD to which you can record only once, or a rewritable DVD to which you can record and then re-record data. Recordable DVDs come in two formats, **DVD-R** and **DVD+R**, and likewise re-recordable DVDs come in two formats, **DVD-RW** and **DVD+RW**. DVD drives on new computers are capable of reading from and writing to both -RW and +RW DVDs and CDs, as well as DVDs with two layers. **BD-R** are Blu-ray discs that you can record to once, and **BD-RE** are Blu-ray discs that you can record to multiple times. You need a Blu-ray drive to use Blu-ray discs.

Examining Input Devices

Before a computer can produce useful information, people must get data into the computer. This is accomplished by using input devices. In a typical personal computer system, you input data and commands by using an **input device** such as a keyboard or a mouse. Computers can also receive input from a storage device. You will learn about storage devices later in this unit. As Kevin explains peripheral devices to the Sheehan Tours staff, they ask several questions about input devices. For example, one person doesn't understand the difference between a mouse and a trackball. Kevin continues his explanation with a discussion of various input devices.

There are many types of input devices, as described below:

QUICK TIP

Another way to avoid repetitive motion injuries is to take frequent breaks when working at a computer and stretch your hands and wrists.

- One of the most frequently used input devices is a **keyboard**. The top keyboard in Figure A-11 is a standard keyboard. The bottom keyboard in Figure A-11 is **ergonomic**, which means that it has been designed to fit the natural placement of your hands and should reduce the risk of repetitive-motion injuries. Many keyboards, like the ones shown, have additional keys programmed as shortcut keys to commonly used functions.

- Another common input device is a **pointing device**, which controls the **pointer**, a small arrow or other symbol on the screen. Pointing devices are used to select commands and manipulate text or graphics on the screen.

    - The most popular pointing device for a desktop computer is a **mouse**, such as the one shown on the left side in Figure A-12. An ordinary mouse has a rolling ball on its underside, and an optical mouse has a tiny camera on its underside that takes pictures as the mouse is moved. You control the pointer by moving the entire mouse. A mouse usually has two or more buttons for clicking commands. A mouse might also have a **scroll wheel** that you roll to scroll the page on the screen and that may function as one of the buttons.

    - The **trackball**, such as the one shown on the right side in Figure A-12, is similar to a mouse except that the rolling ball is on the top side and you control the movement of the pointer by moving only the ball.

    - Notebook computers are usually equipped with a touch pad or a pointing stick. See Figure A-13. A **touch pad** is a touch-sensitive device that you drag your finger over to control the pointer. The buttons are located at the bottom of the touch pad. A **pointing stick** is a small device that looks like a pencil eraser embedded among the typing keys that you push up, left, right, or down to move the pointer. Two buttons equivalent to mouse buttons are located in front of the spacebar on the keyboard.

- A **touchscreen** is a display that while showing you the output, allows you to touch it with your finger or a stylus to input commands. Touchscreens are found on some ATMs, smartphones, and MP3 players. Tablet PCs and slate computers use touchscreen technology, and the newest operating system from Microsoft, Windows 7, supports touchscreens.

- A **scanner** is a device that transfers the content on a piece of paper into memory. To do this, you place a piece of paper on the glass, a beam of light moves across the glass similar to a photocopier, and stores the image or words on the paper as digital information. You can scan a document or a photo and save it as an image file, or you can scan a document and have the text "read" by the scanner and saved in a document file for editing later.

- Microphones are another type of input device. You can use them to record sound for certain types of files, or, if you have the voice-recognition software, you can use them to input data and commands.

- Input devices can be connected to the computer with cables or wirelessly. Wireless input devices connect to the computer using infrared or radio frequency technology, similar to a remote control for a television.

Understanding assistive devices

People with physical impairments or disabilities can use computers because of advances in making computers accessible to everyone. For example, people who cannot use their arms or hands instead can use foot, head, or eye movements to control the pointer. People with poor vision can use keyboards with large keys for input, screen enlargers to enlarge the type and images on the monitor, or screen readers to read the content of the screen aloud. Computers have even been developed that can be controlled by a person's thoughts, that is, the brain's electromagnetic waves.

FIGURE A-11: Keyboards

Shortcut keys to commonly used functions

FIGURE A-12: Personal computer pointing devices

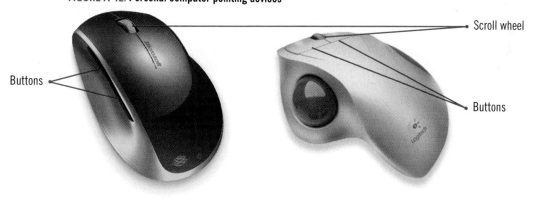

Scroll wheel

Buttons

Buttons

FIGURE A-13: Notebook pointing devices

Touch pad

Pointing stick

Examining Output Devices

As stated earlier, output is the result of processing data; **output devices** show you those results. The most commonly used output devices are monitors and printers. Kevin continues his discussion of peripheral devices with an explanation of output devices.

Output devices are described below:

- The **monitor** displays the output from a computer.

  - The monitor shown in Figure A-14 is a **flat panel monitor**, a lightweight monitor that takes up very little room on the desktop. Most flat panel monitors use **LCD (liquid crystal display)** technology, which creates the image you see on the screen by manipulating light within a layer of liquid crystal. LCD monitors require a backlight. Flat-panel monitors labeled as **LED (light emitting diode)** monitors use LEDs to provide the backlight. LED backlighting is more energy efficient than ordinary backlighting.
  - Monitor **screen size** is the diagonal measurement from one corner of the screen to the other. In general, monitors on desktop computers range in size from 15" to 30", whereas monitors on notebook computers range in size from 12" to 20".
  - Most monitors have a **graphics display**, which divides the screen into a matrix of small dots called **pixels**. **Resolution** is the number of pixels the monitor displays. Standard resolutions range from 640 × 480 to 1920 × 1200. If your screen is small, a 1600 × 1200 resolution will make the objects on the screen too small to see clearly. **Dot pitch (dp)** measures the distance between pixels, so a smaller dot pitch means a sharper image. A .28 or .26 dot pitch is typical for today's monitors.
  - To display graphics, a computer must have a **graphics card**, also called a **video display adapter** or **video card**, or a built-in **graphics processor** (sometimes called a **built-in graphics card**). The graphics card or processor controls the signals the computer sends to the monitor.

- A **printer** produces a paper copy, often called **hard copy**, of the text or graphics processed by the computer. There are three popular categories of printers: laser printers, inkjet printers, and dot matrix printers.

  - **Laser printers**, like the one shown on the left in Figure A-15, are popular for business use because they produce high-quality output quickly and efficiently. In a laser printer, a temporary laser image is transferred onto paper with a powdery substance called **toner**.
  - **Inkjet printers**, such as the one shown on the right in Figure A-15, are popular printers for home use. These printers spray ink onto paper and produce output whose quality is comparable to that of a laser printer.
  - **Dot matrix printers** transfer ink to the paper by striking a ribbon with pins. A 24-pin dot matrix printer produces better quality print than a 9-pin. Dot matrix printers are most often used when a large number of pages need to be printed fairly quickly or when a business needs to print multi-page continuous forms.

- Speakers allow you to hear sounds from the computer. Speakers can be separate peripheral devices attached to the computer, or they can be built in to the monitor. For speakers to work, a sound card must be installed on the motherboard. The sound card converts sounds so that they can be broadcast through speakers.

FIGURE A-14: LCD monitor

FIGURE A-15: Printers

Laser printer

Inkjet printer

Concepts 2010

Exploring Data Communications

Data communications is the transmission of data from one computer to another or to a peripheral device. The computer that originates the message is the **sender**. The message is sent over some type of **channel**, such as a telephone or coaxial cable. The computer or device at the message's destination is the **receiver**. The rules that establish an orderly transfer of data between the sender and the receiver are called **protocols**. The transmission protocol between a computer and its peripheral devices is handled by a **device driver**, or simply **driver**, which is a computer program that can establish communication because it contains information about the characteristics of your computer and of the device. 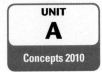 The Sheehan Tours staff will use their computers to connect to the computers at the Quest headquarters in California as well as to surf the Internet, so Kevin next explains how computers communicate.

The following describes some of the ways that computers communicate:

- The data path between the microprocessor, RAM, and the peripherals along which communication travels is called the **data bus**.

- An external peripheral device must have a corresponding **expansion port** and **cable** that connect it to the computer. Inside the computer, each port connects to a **controller card**, sometimes called an **expansion card** or **interface card**. These cards plug into electrical connectors on the motherboard called **expansion slots** or **slots**. Personal computers can have several types of ports, including parallel, serial, SCSI, USB, MIDI, and Ethernet. Figure A-16 shows the ports on one desktop personal computer.

- A **USB (Universal Serial Bus) port** is a high-speed serial port which allows multiple connections at the same port. The device you install must have a **USB connector**, a small rectangular plug, as shown in Figure A-17. When you plug the USB connector into the USB port, the computer recognizes the device and allows you to use it immediately. USB flash storage devices plug into USB ports. For most USB devices, power is supplied via the port, so there is no need for extra power cables.

- Another standard for transferring information between digital devices similar to USB is FireWire. **FireWire** was developed by Apple Computer company and the Institute of Electrical and Electronics Engineers (IEEE) standardized the technology as the **IEEE 1394 interface**. Data transfers are significantly faster using this type of connection than using a USB connection.

- Monitors are connected to computers through HDMI, DVI, or VGA ports. **HDMI (high-definition multimedia interface)** transmits video and audio digitally, **DVI (digital video interface)** transmits video digitally, and **VGA (video graphics array)** allows analog video transmission.

- Speakers and a microphone connect to a computer via ports on the sound card.

- A keyboard and a mouse connect via **PS/2 ports** or USB ports. A wireless keyboard or mouse connects via a special connector that plugs into a USB port. Printers also connect via a USB port.

- You can connect to another computer, a LAN, a **modem** (a device that connects your computer to a standard telephone jack or to a cable connection), or sometimes directly to the Internet using an **Ethernet port**. Ethernet ports allow data to be transmitted at high speeds.

FIGURE A-16: Computer expansion ports

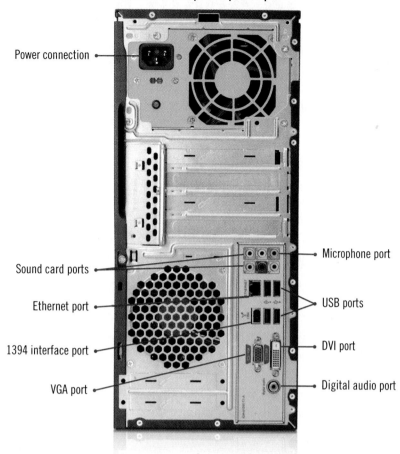

Power connection

Sound card ports

Ethernet port

1394 interface port

VGA port

Microphone port

USB ports

DVI port

Digital audio port

FIGURE A-17: USB connector

Understanding Essential Computer Concepts

Learning about Networks

A **network** connects one computer to other computers and peripheral devices, enabling you to share data and resources with others. There are a variety of network configurations; however, any type of network has some basic characteristics and requirements that you should know. ▨▨▨▨ Kevin continues his discussion of how computers communicate with an explanation of networking.

DETAILS

Components of networks and the types of networks are described below:

- Each computer that is part of the network must have a **network interface card (NIC)** installed. This card creates a communications channel between the computer and the network. A cable is used to connect the NIC port to the network.

- **Network software** is also essential, establishing the communications protocols that will be observed on the network and controlling the "traffic flow" as data travels throughout the network.

- Some networks have one or more computers, called **servers**, that act as the central storage location for programs and provide mass storage for most of the data used on the network. A network with a server and computers dependent on the server is called a **client/server network**. The dependent computers are the **clients**.

- When a network does not have a server, all the computers essentially are equal, and programs and data are distributed among them. This is called a **peer-to-peer network**.

- A personal computer that is not connected to a network is called a **standalone computer**. When it is connected to the network, it becomes a **workstation**. Any device connected to the network is called a **node**. A **router** is a device that controls traffic between network components. Figure A-18 illustrates a typical network configuration.

- In a **local area network (LAN)**, computers and peripheral devices are located relatively close to each other, generally in the same building.

QUICK TIP
The **World Wide Web** is subset of the Internet, and is a huge database of information stored on network servers.

- A **wide area network (WAN)** is more than one LAN connected together. The **Internet** is the largest example of a WAN.

- In a **wireless local area network (WLAN)**, computers and peripherals use high-frequency radio waves instead of wires to communicate and connect in a network. **Wi-Fi** (short for **wireless fidelity**) is the term created by the nonprofit Wi-Fi Alliance to describe networks connected using a standard radio frequency established by the Institute of Electrical and Electronics Engineers (IEEE). Wi-Fi is used over short distances to connect computers to a LAN.

- A **personal area network (PAN)** is a network that allows two or more devices located close to each other to communicate or to connect a device to the Internet. In a PAN, devices are connected with cables or wireless.
  - **Infrared technology** uses infrared light waves to beam data from one device to another. The devices must be compatible, and they must be positioned close to each other with their infrared ports pointed at each other to communicate. This is the technology used in TV remote controls.
  - **Bluetooth** uses short range radio waves to connect a device wirelessly to another device or to the Internet. The devices must each have a Bluetooth transmitter, but unlike infrared connections, they can communicate around corners or through walls.

- **WiMAX** (short for **Worldwide Interoperability for Microwave Access**), another standard defined by the IEEE, allows computer users to connect over many miles to a LAN. A WiMAX tower sends signals to a WiMAX receiver built or plugged into a computer. WiMAX towers can communicate with each other or with a company that provides connections to the Internet.

FIGURE A-18: Typical network configuration

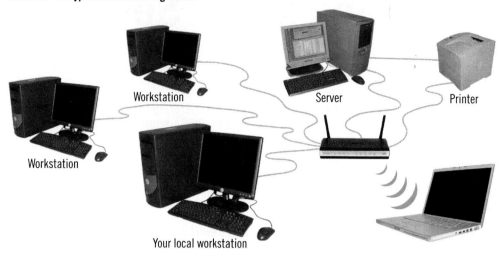

Workstation

Workstation

Server

Printer

Your local workstation

Understanding telecommunications

Telecommunications means communicating over a comparatively long distance using a phone line or some other data conduit. To make this connection, you must use a modem. Modem stands for *mo*dulator-*dem*odulator. The modem converts the **digital**, or stop-start, **signals** your computer outputs into **analog**, or continuous wave, **signals** (sound waves) that can traverse ordinary phone lines. Figure A-19 shows the telecommunications process, in which a modem converts digital signals to analog signals at the sending site (modulates) and a second modem converts the analog signals back into digital signals at the receiving site (demodulates). Most computers today come with a built-in 56 K modem and NIC (network interface card). 56 K represents the modem's capability to send and receive about 56,000 **bits per second (bps)**. People who want to use a high-speed connection either over phone lines, such as a **DSL (digital subscriber line)**, or over a cable connection, usually need to purchase an external DSL or cable modem separately. High-speed connections are often called **broadband connections**.

FIGURE A-19: Using modems to send and receive data

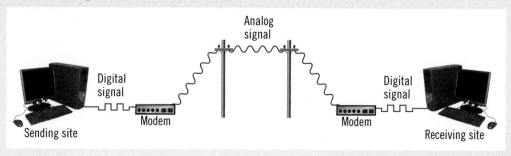

Analog signal

Digital signal

Modem

Sending site

Digital signal

Modem

Receiving site

Learning about Security Threats

Security refers to the steps a computer owner takes to prevent unauthorized use of or damage to the computer. Once a computer is connected to a network, it is essential that the computer be protected against possible threats from people intent on stealing information or causing malicious damage. ▆▆▆▆ Kevin explains how important it is to be vigilant about keeping the office computers secure and reviews ways to do this.

DETAILS

Several types of security threats are discussed below:

- **Malware** is a broad term that describes any program that is intended to cause harm or convey information to others without the owner's permission.

QUICK TIP

Some specific types of viruses are called worms; another type is a Trojan horse. Antivirus software usually protects against both types.

  - Unscrupulous programmers deliberately construct harmful programs, called **viruses**, which instruct your computer to perform destructive activities, such as erasing a disk drive. Some viruses are more annoying than destructive, but some can be harmful, erasing data or causing your hard disk to require reformatting. **Antivirus software**, sometimes referred to as **virus protection software**, searches executable files for the sequences of characters that may cause harm and disinfects the files by erasing or disabling those commands. Figure A-20 shows the dialog box that appears when the Trend Micro antivirus program is scanning a computer for potential threats.

QUICK TIP

Adware is software installed with another program usually with the user's permission that generates advertising revenue for the program's creator by displaying ads targeted to the program's user.

  - Some software programs contain other programs called **spyware** that track a computer user's Internet usage and send this data back to the company or person that created it. Most often, this is done without the computer user's permission or knowledge. **Anti-spyware software** can detect these programs and delete them.

- A **firewall** is like a locked door on your computer. It prevents other computers on the Internet from accessing your computer and prevents programs on it from accessing the Internet without your permission. A firewall can be either hardware or software.

  - A hardware firewall provides strong protection against incoming threats. A router usually has a built-in firewall.
  - Software firewalls track all incoming and outgoing traffic. If a program that never accessed the Internet before attempts to do so, the user is notified and can choose to forbid access. There are several free software firewall packages available.

- Criminals are getting more aggressive as they try to figure out new ways to access computer users' personal information and passwords.

  - A Web site set up to look exactly like another Web site, such as a bank's Web site, but which does not actually belong to the organization portrayed in the site, is a **spoofed** site. The site developer creates a **URL** (address on the Web) that looks similar to a URL from the legitimate site. Usually, spoofed sites are set up to try to convince customers of the real site to enter personal information, such as credit card numbers, Social Security numbers, and passwords, so that the thief collecting the information can use it to steal the customer's money or identity. Figure A-21 shows the alert displayed in the Internet Explorer browser when a known spoofed site is visited.

QUICK TIP

Never click a URL in a suspected phishing message. Open your browser and type the URL of the organization into the Address or Location bar instead.

  - **Phishing** refers to the practice of sending e-mails to customers or potential customers of a legitimate Web site asking them to click a link in the e-mail. If you click the link, your **browser** (the software you use to access Web sites) displaying the spoofed site where the user is asked to verify or enter personal information.
  - Sometimes a criminal can break into a **DNS server** (a computer responsible for directing Internet traffic) and redirect any attempts to access a particular Web site to the criminal's spoofed site. This is called **pharming**.

FIGURE A-20: Antivirus scan in progress

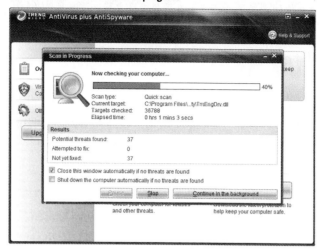

FIGURE A-21: The Internet Explorer browser when visiting a known spoofed site

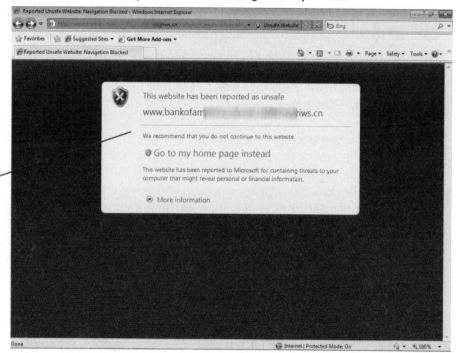

Message warns you that the website has been reported as unsafe

Protecting information with passwords

You can protect data on your computer by using passwords. You can set up accounts on your computer for multiple users and require that users sign in with a username and password before they can use the computer. This is known as **logging in** or **logging on**. You can also protect individual files on your computer so that people who try to open or alter a file need to type the password before they are allowed access to the file. Many Web sites require a username and password to access the information stored on it. To prevent anyone from guessing your passwords, you should always create and use strong passwords. A **strong password** consists of at least eight characters of upper- and lowercase letters and numbers. Avoid using common personal information, such as birthdays and addresses, in your password.

Understanding System Software

Sometimes the term software refers to a single program, but often the term refers to a collection of programs and data that are packaged together. **System software** helps the computer carry out its basic operating tasks. 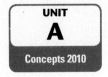 Before Kevin describes the various types of software that people use to accomplish things like writing memos, he needs to describe system software.

The components of system software are described below:

- System software manages the fundamental operations of your computer, such as loading programs and data into memory, executing programs, saving data to disks, displaying information on the monitor, and transmitting data through a port to a peripheral device. There are four types of system software: operating systems, utilities, device drivers, and programming languages.

- Recall that an **operating system** allocates system resources, manages storage space, maintains security, detects equipment failure, and controls basic input and output. **Input and output**, or **I/O**, is the flow of data from the microprocessor to memory to peripherals and back again.

  - The operating system allocates system resources so programs run properly. A **system resource** is any part of the computer system, including memory, storage devices, and the microprocessor, that can be used by a computer program.
  - The operating system is also responsible for managing the files on your storage devices. Not only does it open and save files, but it also keeps track of every part of every file for you and lets you know if any part is missing.
  - While you are working on the computer, the operating system is constantly guarding against equipment failure. Each electronic circuit is checked periodically, and the moment a problem is detected, the user is notified with a warning message on the screen.
  - Microsoft Windows, used on many personal computers, and the MAC OS, used exclusively on Macintosh computers, are referred to as **operating environments** because they provide a **graphical user interface** (**GUI**, pronounced "goo-ey") that acts as a liaison between the user and all of the computer's hardware and software. Figure A-22 shows the starting screen on a computer using Microsoft Windows 7.

- **Utilities** are another category of system software that augment the operating system by taking over some of its responsibility for allocating hardware resources.

- As you learned earlier in the discussion of ports, device drivers handle the transmission protocol between a computer and its peripherals. When you add a device to an existing computer, part of its installation includes adding its device driver to the computer's configuration.

- Computer **programming languages**, which a programmer uses to write computer instructions, are also part of the system software. The instructions are translated into electrical signals that the computer can manipulate and process.

FIGURE A-22: Windows 7 starting screen

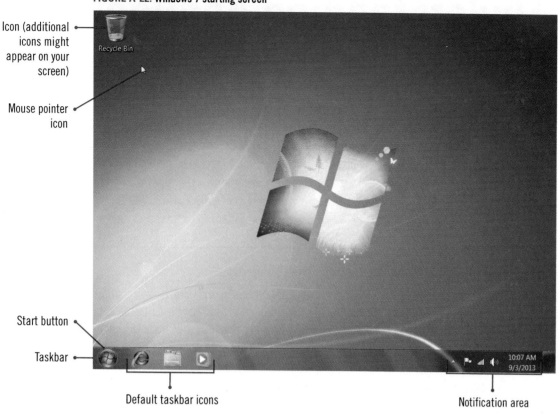

Icon (additional icons might appear on your screen)

Mouse pointer icon

Start button

Taskbar

Default taskbar icons

Notification area

Examining Windows 7 hardware requirements

Windows 7, the newest version of the Windows operating system, requires a computer with at least a 1 GHz processor, 1 GB of RAM for the 32-bit version or 2 GB of RAM for the 64-bit version, a DirectX 9 graphics processor, 128 MB of specialized graphics RAM, and 16 GB of available space for the 32-bit version or 20 GB for the 64-bit version. Keep in mind that these are the minimum recommendations. To prevent your computer from slowing to a crawl, you should consider upgrading the amount of RAM and the processor speed.

Concepts 2010

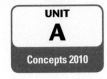
Understanding Application Software

Application software enables you to perform specific computer tasks. Many programs allow users to use data created in one application in a document created by another application. **Object linking and embedding (OLE)** refers to the ability to use data from another file, called the **source**. **Embedding** occurs when you copy and paste the source data in the new file. **Linking** allows you to create a connection between the source data and the copy in the new file. The link updates the copy every time a change is made to the source data. The seamless nature of OLE among some applications is referred to as **integration**. ▰▰▰ Now that the Sheehan Tours staff understands system software, Kevin describes some common application software.

Typical application software includes the following:

QUICK TIP

Most document production software allows you to perform **copy-and-paste** and **cut-and-paste operations**, to duplicate or move words around.

- **Document production software** includes word processing software, desktop publishing software, e-mail editors, and Web authoring software. All of these production tools have a variety of features that assist you in writing and formatting documents, including changing the **font** (the style of type) or adding color and design elements. Most offer **spell checking** to help you avoid typographical and spelling errors, as shown in Figure A-23.

- **Spreadsheet software** is a numerical analysis tool. Spreadsheet software creates a **worksheet**, composed of a grid of columns and rows. You can type data into the cells, and then enter mathematical formulas into other cells that reference the data. Figure A-24 shows a typical worksheet that includes a simple calculation and the data in the spreadsheet represented as a simple graph.

- **Database management software** lets you collect and manage data. A **database** is a collection of information stored on one or more computers organized in a uniform format of records and fields. A **record** is a collection of data items in a database. A **field** is one piece of information in the record. An example of a database is the online catalog of books at a library; the catalog contains one record for each book in the library, and each record contains fields that identify the title, the author, and the subjects under which the book can be classified.

- **Graphics** and **presentation software** allow you to create illustrations, diagrams, graphs, and charts that can be projected before a group, printed out for quick reference, or transmitted to remote computers. You can also use **clip art**, simple drawings that are included as collections with many software packages.

- **Photo editing software** allows you to manipulate digital photos. You can make the images brighter, add special effects, add other images, or crop the photo to include only relevant parts of the image. Examples of photo editing software are Adobe Photoshop and Picasa. **Video editing software**, such as Windows Live Movie Maker or Adobe Premier, allows you to edit video by clipping it, adding captions and a soundtrack, or rearranging clips.

- **Multimedia authoring software** allows you to record digital sound files, video files, and animations that can be included in presentations and other documents.

QUICK TIP

Some information management software allows you to synchronize information between a PDA and a desktop or notebook computer.

- **Information management software** keeps track of schedules, appointments, contacts, and "to-do" lists. Most e-mail software allows users to add all the information about contacts to the list of e-mail addresses. In addition, some software, such as Microsoft Outlook, combines a contact list with information management components, such as a calendar and to-do list.

- **Web site creation and management software** allows you to create and manage Web sites. They allow you to see what the Web pages will look like as you create them.

FIGURE A-23: Checking the spelling in a document

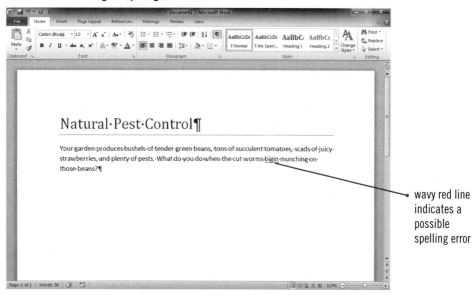

wavy red line
indicates a
possible
spelling error

FIGURE A-24: Typical worksheet with numerical data and a graph

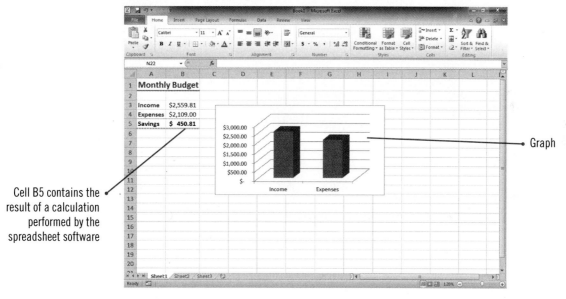

Graph

Cell B5 contains the
result of a calculation
performed by the
spreadsheet software

Computing in the cloud

Cloud computing means that data, applications, and even resources are stored on servers accessed over the Internet rather than on users' computers, and you access only what you need when you need it. Many individuals and companies are moving towards "the cloud" for at least some of their needs. For example, some companies provide space and computing power to developers for a fee. Individuals might subscribe to a backup service such as Carbonite or Mozy so that their data is automatically backed up on a computer at the physical location of those companies. Google Docs and Microsoft Web Apps provide both free and paid versions of various applications that you access by logging in to their Web sites. For now, these applications are not as robust as the applications you install on your own machine, but that is likely to change in the future.

Practice

For current SAM information, including versions and content details, visit SAM Central (http://www.cengage.com/samcentral). If you have a SAM user profile, you may have access to hands-on instruction, practice, and assessment of the skills covered in this unit. Since various versions of SAM are supported throughout the life of this text, check with your instructor for the correct instructions and URL/Web site for accessing assignments.

Concepts Review

Match the statements with the elements labeled in the screen shown in Figure A-25.

FIGURE A-25

1. Which component is used to enter text?
2. Which component do you use to point to items on the screen?
3. Which component processes data?
4. Which component displays output?

Understanding Essential Computer Concepts

Match each term with the statement that best describes it.

5. netbook
6. commands
7. byte
8. RAM
9. hard disk
10. expansion slot
11. server
12. spyware
13. operating system
14. database

a. Temporarily holds data and programs while the computer is on
b. A type of subnotebook computer that is primarily designed to allow users to access the Internet and check e-mail
c. Magnetic storage media that is usually sealed in a case inside the computer
d. A collection of information stored on one or more computers organized in a uniform format of records and fields
e. Series of eight bits
f. A computer on a network that acts as the central storage location for programs and data used on the network
g. Software that allocates resources, manages storage space, maintains security, and controls I/O
h. A program that tracks a user's Internet usage without the user's permission
i. A slot on the motherboard into which a controller card for a peripheral device is inserted
j. Input instructions that tell the computer how to process data

Select the best answer from the list of choices.

15. **Which one of the following would not be considered a personal computer?**
   a. Desktop
   b. Mainframe
   c. Notebook
   d. Tablet PC

16. **The intangible components of a computer system, including the programs, are called:**
   a. peripherals
   b. hardware
   c. software
   d. price

17. **What part of the computer is responsible for executing instructions to process information?**
   a. Peripheral device
   b. Card
   c. Motherboard
   d. Processor

18. **What are the technical details about each hardware component called?**
   a. Configuration
   b. Specifications
   c. Circuits
   d. Cards

19. **Keyboards, monitors, and printers are all examples of which of the following?**
   a. Peripheral devices
   b. Input devices
   c. Output devices
   d. Software

20. **Which of the following is a pointing device that allows you to control the pointer by moving the entire device around on a desk?**
   a. Mouse
   b. Trackball
   c. Touch pad
   d. Pointing stick

21. **In order to display graphics, a computer needs a monitor and a(n):**
   a. expansion port
   b. graphics card or processor
   c. network card (NIC)
   d. sound card

22. **What do you call each 1 or 0 used in the representation of computer data?**
   a. An ASCII
   b. A pixel
   c. A bit
   d. A byte

23. **What is a megabyte?**
    a. 10 kilobytes
    b. About a million bytes
    c. One-half a gigabyte
    d. About a million bits

24. **Which of the following permanently stores the set of instructions that the computer uses to activate the software that controls the processing function when you turn the computer on?**
    a. RAM
    b. ROM
    c. The hard disk
    d. CPU cache

25. **Which of the following is space on the computer's storage devices that simulates additional RAM?**
    a. Read-only memory
    b. Cache memory
    c. Volatile memory
    d. Virtual memory

26. **Which of the following temporarily stores data and programs while you are using them?**
    a. RAM
    b. ROM
    c. The hard disk
    d. CPU cache

27. **Which of the following is not a permanent storage medium?**
    a. Hard disk
    b. Optical disk
    c. DVD
    d. RAM

28. **The transmission protocol between a computer and its peripheral devices is handled by a:**
    a. driver
    b. controller card
    c. channel
    d. data bus

29. **Which of the following is the data path between the microprocessor, RAM, and the peripherals?**
    a. Cable
    b. Data bus
    c. Data channel
    d. Data port

30. **The computer that originates a message to send to another computer is called the:**
    a. channel
    b. sender
    c. receiver
    d. driver

31. **A personal computer that is connected to a network is called a:**
    a. netbook
    b. desktop
    c. workstation
    d. channel

32. **Which of the following acts as a locked door on a computer?**
    a. DNS server
    b. Antivirus software
    c. Spyware
    d. Firewall

33. **A _____ consists of connected computers and peripheral devices that are located relatively close to each other.**
    a. PAN
    b. LAN
    c. WAN
    d. WLAN

34. **When data, applications, and resources are stored on servers rather than on users' computers, it is referred to as _____.**
    a. sky computing
    b. cloud computing
    c. shared computing
    d. leased computing

35. **A Web site set up to look exactly like another Web site, such as a bank's Web site, but which does not actually belong to the organization portrayed in the site, is a _____ site.**
    a. phished
    b. spoofed
    c. served
    d. malware

Independent Challenge 1

This Independent Challenge requires an Internet connection.

In order to run the newest software, many people need to upgrade their existing computer system or buy a brand new one. What do you do with your old computer when you purchase a new one? Most municipalities have enacted laws regulating the disposal of electronics. Research these laws in your city and state and write a brief report describing them.

a. Start your browser, go to your favorite search engine, and then search for information about laws regarding the disposal of electronics in your city and state. Try finding your city's Web site and searching it for the information, or use **electronics disposal laws** followed by your city name as a search term and then repeat that search with your state's name in place of your city's name.

b. Open each Web site that you find in a separate tab or browser window.

c. Read the information on each Web site. Can some components be thrown away? Are there laws that apply only to monitors? Are there different laws for individuals and businesses? Does the size of the business matter? Are manufacturers or resellers required to accept used components that they manufactured or sold?

Advanced Challenge Exercise

- Search for organizations to which you can donate your computer.
- How do these organizations promise to protect your privacy?
- Can you take a deduction on your federal income tax for your donation?

d. Write a short report describing your findings. Include the URLs for all relevant Web sites. (*Hint*: If you are using a word processor to write your report, you can copy the URLs from your browser and paste them into the document. Drag to select the entire URL in the Address or Location bar in your browser. Right-click the selected text, then click Copy on the shortcut menu. Position the insertion point in the document where you want the URL to appear, then press [Ctrl][V].)

Independent Challenge 2

This Independent Challenge requires an Internet connection.

New viruses are discovered on an almost daily basis. If you surf the Internet or exchange e-mail, it is important to use updated anti-virus software. Research the most current virus threats and create a table listing the threats and details about them.

   a. Start your browser, go to Trend Micro's Web site at **www.trendmicro.com**, and then click the TrendWatch link under the Threat Meter. On the TrendWatch page, click the Current Threat Activity link, click the Malware & Vulnerability Information link, and then click the View the Malware Map link. (If you don't see that link, type **Malware Map** in the Search box on the page, then click the link to Malware Map in the list of search results.)

   b. Click links to the top five threats, and then read the description of each threat. The pages describing the threats might open in a new tab.

   c. Open a new word processing document and create a table listing each virus threat, a description of what each virus does, how widely each virus is distributed based on the number of infected computers, and how damaging each virus is (the Risk level).

   d. In your browser, go to the Security Advisor on CA's Web site at **www3.ca.com/securityadvisor**, and then click the Virus Information Center link. If any of the top five virus threats are different from the ones on the Trend Micro site, add them to your table. (*Hint*: After you click a virus name, check the "Also known as" list.)

   e. For any viruses that are already in your table because they were on the Trend Micro site, read the CA description to see if there is any additional information describing how the virus could damage your system. Add this information to your table.

Independent Challenge 3

This Independent Challenge requires an Internet connection.

One of the keyboards shown in this unit is an ergonomic keyboard. Ergonomics is the study of the design of a workspace so that the worker can work efficiently and avoid injury. The U.S. Occupational Safety and Health Administration (OSHA) has developed guidelines that describe a healthy computer work environment. Research these guidelines and evaluate your workspace.

a. Start your browser, and then go to **www.osha.gov/SLTC/etools/computerworkstations**.

b. Read the information on the main page. Follow links to descriptions of the best arrangement for equipment you use when working on a computer. (*Hint*: Look for the Workstation Components link, and point to it to open a submenu of links.)

c. Locate and print the checklist for evaluating your workspace. (*Hint*: Click the Checklist link, then click the View/Print the Evaluation Checklist PDF link. A new tab or window opens and the checklist opens in Adobe Acrobat Reader, a program that displays PDF files. If a dialog box opens telling you that you need to install Acrobat Reader to continue, ask your instructor or technical support person for help.)

d. Using the checklist, evaluate each of the conditions listed. If a condition does not apply to you, write N/A (not applicable) in the Yes column.

Advanced Challenge Exercise

- Use the OSHA Web site or a search engine to research repetitive motion injuries to which computer users are susceptible.
- Evaluate your risk for at least three common injuries.
- On the OSHA checklist, note what injury or injuries each applicable item or behavior will help prevent.

Real Life Independent Challenge

You are buying a new desktop computer. You want the computer to run Windows 7 and Microsoft Office 2010, and you want to make sure you are protected against security threats. You would like a large flat panel monitor and you need a printer. However, you have a limited budget, and can spend no more than $800 for everything (all hardware and software).

a. To help you organize your information, create the table shown in Figure A-26.

FIGURE A-26

	Your Requirements	Computer Retailer #1	Computer Retailer #2	Computer Retailer #3
Windows 7 (Edition)				
Office 2010 (Edition)				
Brand of computer				
Processor (brand and speed)				
RAM (amount)				
Video RAM (amount)				
Hard disk (size)				
Monitor (type and size)				
Printer (type and speed)				
Speakers				
Antivirus software				
Firewall (software or router with built-in firewall)				
System price				
Additional costs				
Total price				

b. Decide which edition of Windows 7 you want, and enter it in the Your Requirements column of the table. To read a description of the available editions, go to www.microsoft.com and search the Microsoft Web site for information about the Windows 7 Editions.

c. Research the hardware requirements for running the edition of Windows 7 you selected. Search the Microsoft Web site again for the minimum and recommended hardware requirements for running Windows 7.

d. Decide which edition of Office 2010 you want and enter it in the first column of the table. Search the Microsoft Web site to find a description of the software included with each edition of Office 2010, and then search for the hardware requirements for running the edition of Office 2010 that you chose. If necessary, change the hardware requirements in the table.

e. Research the cost of your new computer system. To begin, visit local stores, look at advertisements, or search the Web for computer system retailers. Most computer retailers sell complete systems that come with all the necessary hardware, an operating system, and additional software already installed. In the Computer Retailer #1 column of the table, fill in the specifications for the system you chose. If any item listed as a minimum requirement is not included with the system you chose, find the cost of adding that item and enter the price in the table. Repeat this process with systems from two other retailers, entering the specifications in the Computer Retailer #2 and Computer Retailer #3 columns.

f. If the system you chose does not come with a printer, search the Web for an inexpensive color inkjet printer.

g. If the system you chose does not come with antivirus software, search the Web for the cost, if any, of an antivirus software package. Make sure you look up reviews of the package you chose. Decide whether to purchase this software or download a free one, and enter this cost in the table.

h. If you decide you need a router with a built-in firewall, search the Web for the price of one. Enter this information in the table.

i. Total the costs you entered in the table for the various items. Is the total cost $800 or less? If not, revisit some of the items. Can you get a less expensive printer? Do you need to downgrade to a less expensive monitor? Likewise, if you are under budget, upgrade a part of your system; perhaps you can afford to upgrade the monitor to a larger, flat panel monitor. Reevaluate your choices if necessary and try to get your total cost close to $800.

Glossary

Adware Software installed with another program that generates advertising revenue for the program's creator by displaying targeted ads to the program's user.

American Standard Code for Information Interchange *See* ASCII.

Analog signal A continuous wave signal (sound wave) that can traverse ordinary phone lines.

Anti-spyware software Software that detects and removes spyware.

Antivirus software Software that searches executable files for the sequences of characters that may cause harm and disinfects the files by erasing or disabling those commands. *Also called* virus protection software.

Application software Software that enables you to perform specific computer tasks, such as document production, spreadsheet calculations, database management, and presentation preparation.

Architecture The design and construction of a computer; *also called* configuration.

ASCII (American Standard Code for Information Interchange) The number system that personal computers use to represent character data.

BD-R A Blu-ray disc on which you can record data once.

BD-RE A Blu-ray disc on which you can record data as on a BD-R, and then delete or re-record data on it as needed.

BIOS Stands for basic input/output system, the set of instructions stored in ROM that the computer uses to check its components to ensure they are working and to activate the software that provides the basic functionality of the computer when you turn on the computer.

Binary digit (bit) The representation of data as a 1 or 0.

Bit *See* binary digit.

Bits per second (bps) The unit of measurement for the speed of data transmission.

Bluetooth A wireless technology standard that allows electronic devices to use short range radio waves to communicate with one another or connect to the Internet; the radio waves can be transmitted around corners and through walls.

Blu-ray A disc used for storing high-definition video that stores 25 GB of data per layer.

Boot process The set of events that occurs between the moment you turn on the computer and the moment you can begin to use the computer.

Boot up The act of turning on the computer.

Bps *See* bits per second.

Broadband connection A high-speed connection to the Internet.

Browser Software that you use to navigate the World Wide Web and display information on Web sites.

Built-in graphics card *See* graphics processor.

Byte A series of eight bits.

Cable Plastic-enclosed wires that attach a peripheral device to a computer port.

Cache memory Special high-speed memory chips on the motherboard or CPU that store frequently-accessed and recently-accessed data and commands; *also called* RAM cache or CPU cache.

Card A removable circuit board that is inserted into a slot in the motherboard to expand the capabilities of the motherboard.

CD (compact disc) An optical storage device that can store 700 MB of data.

CD-R (compact disc recordable) A CD that on which you can record data with a laser that changes the reflectivity of a dye layer on the blank disk, creating dark spots on the disk's surface that represent the data; once the data is recorded, you cannot erase or modify it.

CD-ROM (compact disc read-only memory) A CD that contains software or music when you purchase it, but you cannot record additional data on it.

CD-RW (compact disc rewritable) A CD on which you can record data as on a CD-R, and then delete or re-record data on it as needed.

Cell The intersection of a row and a column in a worksheet.

Central processing unit (CPU) *See* microprocessor.

Channel The medium, such as telephone or coaxial cable, over which a message is sent in data communications.

Characters per second (cps) The unit of measurement for the speed of dot matrix printers.

Chip An integrated circuit embedded in semiconductor material.

Circuit A path along which an electric current travels.

Circuit board A rigid piece of insulating material with circuits on it that control specific functions.

Client A computer networked to and dependent on a server.

Client/server network A network with a server and computers dependent on the server.

Clip art Simple drawings that are included as collections with many software packages.

Clock speed The pulse of the processor measured in megahertz or gigahertz.

Cloud computing When data, applications, and resources are stored on servers accessed over the Internet or a company's internal network rather than on user's computers.

CMOS *See* complementary metal oxide semiconductor memory.

Command A type of input that instructs the computer how to process data.

Compact disc read-only memory *See* CD-ROM.

Compact disc recordable *See* CD-R.

Compact disk *See* CD.

Compact disk rewritable *See* CD-RW.

Complementary metal oxide semiconductor (CMOS) memory A chip installed on the motherboard powered by a battery whose content changes every time you add or remove hardware on your computer system and that is activated during the boot process so it can identify where essential software is stored. *Also called* semipermanent memory.

Computer An electronic device that accepts input, processes data, displays output, and stores data for retrieval later.

Computer system A computer, its peripheral devices, and software.

Configuration *See* architecture.

Controller card A card that plugs into a slot on the motherboard and connects to a port to provide an electrical connection to a peripheral device. *Also called* expansion card or interface card.

Copy-and-paste operation The feature in document production software that allows you to duplicate selected words and objects somewhere else in the document.

Cps *See* characters per second.

CPU *See* microprocessor.

CPU cache *See* cache memory.

Cut-and-paste operation The feature in document production software that allow you to delete words and objects from one place in a document and place them somewhere else.

Data The words, numbers, figures, sounds, and graphics that describe people, events, things, and ideas.

Data bus The path between the microprocessor, RAM, and the peripherals along which communication travels.

Data communications The transmission of data from one computer to another or to a peripheral device via a channel using a protocol.

Data file A file created by a user, usually with software, such as a report that you write with a word processing program.

Database A collection of information stored on one or more computers organized in a uniform format of records and fields.

Database management software Software you use to collect and manage data.

Desktop computer A personal computer designed to sit compactly on a desk.

Device driver System software that handles the transmission protocol between a computer and its peripheral devices. *Also called* driver.

Digital signal A stop-start signal that your computer outputs.

Digital subscriber line *See* DSL.

DNS server A computer responsible for directing Internet traffic.

Document production software Software, such as word processing software, desktop publishing software, e-mail editors, and Web authoring software, that assists you in writing and formatting documents, including changing the font and checking the spelling.

Dot matrix printer A printer that transfers ink to paper by striking a ribbon with pins.

Dot pitch (dp) The distance between pixels on a monitor.

Dp *See* dot pitch.

Driver *See* device driver.

DSL (digital subscriber line) A high-speed connection over phone lines.

Dual-core processor A CPU that has two processors on the chip.

DVD An optical storage device that can store up to 15.9 GB of data; was originally an acronym for digital video disc and later digital versatile disc.

DVD+R, DVD-R A DVD on which you can record data once.

DVD+RW, DVD-RW A DVD on which you can record data as on a DVD-R, and then delete or re-record data on it as needed.

DVI (digital video interface) port A port that digitally transmits video.

Email An electronic message sent from one user's computer to another.

Embed To copy and paste source data into a new file.

Ergonomic Designed to fit the natural placement of the body to reduce the risk of repetitive-motion injuries.

Ethernet port A port used to connect computers in a LAN or sometimes directly to the Internet; it allows for high-speed data transmission.

Executable file A file that contains the instructions that tell a computer how to perform a specific task, such as the files that are used during the boot process.

Expansion card *See* controller card.

Expansion port The interface between a cable and a controller card. *Also called* port.

Expansion slot An electrical connector on the motherboard into which a card is plugged. *Also called* slot.

Field A piece of information in a record.

File A named collection of stored data.

FireWire A standard for transferring information between digital devices developed by Apple Computer company and the Institute of Electrical and Electronics Engineers (IEEE); was standardized as IEEE 1394 interface.

Firewall Hardware or software that prevents other computers on the Internet from accessing a computer or prevents a program on a computer from accessing the Internet.

Flash drive *See* USB flash storage device.

Flash memory Memory that is similar to ROM except that it can be written to more than once; *also called* solid state storage.

Flash memory card A small, portable cards encased in hard plastic to which data can be written and rewritten.

Flat panel monitor A lightweight monitor that takes up very little room on the desktop and uses LCD technology to create the image on the screen.

Font The style of type.

GB *See* gigabyte.

GHz *See* gigahertz.

Gigabyte (GB) 1,073,741,824 bytes, or about one billion bytes.

Gigahertz (GHz) One billion cycles per second.

Graphical user interface (GUI) A computer environment in which the user manipulates graphics, icons, and dialog boxes to execute commands.

Graphics card A card installed on the motherboard that controls the signals the computer sends to the monitor. *Also called* video display adapter or video card.

Graphics display A monitor that is capable of displaying graphics by dividing the screen into a matrix of pixels.

Graphics processor A processor that controls the signals the computer sends to the monitor. *Also called* built-in graphics card.

Graphics software Software that allows you to create illustrations, diagrams, graphs, and charts.

GUI *See* graphical user interface.

Hand-held computer A small computer designed to fit in the palm of your hand and that generally has fewer capabilities than personal computers.

Hard copy A printed copy of computer output.

Hard disk A magnetic storage device that contains several magnetic oxide-covered metal platters that are usually sealed in a case inside the computer. *Also called* hard disk.

Hardware The physical components of a computer.

HDMI (high-definition multimedia interface) port A port that digitally transmits video and audio.

I/O *See* input and output.

IEEE 1394 interface *See* FireWire.

Information management software Software that keeps track of schedules, appointments, contacts, and "to-do" lists.

Infrared technology A wireless technology in which devices communicate with one another using infrared light waves; the devices must be positioned so that the infrared ports are pointed directly at one another.

Inkjet printer A printer that sprays ink onto paper and produces output whose quality is comparable to that of a laser printer.

Input The data or instructions you type into the computer.

Input and output (I/O) The flow of data from the microprocessor to memory to peripherals and back again.

Input device An instrument, such as a keyboard or a mouse, that you use to enter data and issue commands to the computer.

Integration The seamless nature of OLE among some applications.

Interface card *See* controller card.

Internet The largest network in the world.

K *See* kilobyte.

KB *See* kilobyte.

Keyboard The most frequently used input device; consists of three major parts: the main keyboard, the keypads, and the function keys.

Kilobyte (KB or K) 1,024 bytes, or approximately one thousand bytes.

LAN *See* local area network.

Laptop computer *See* notebook computer.

Laser printer A printer that produces high-quality output quickly and efficiently by transferring a temporary laser image onto paper with toner.

LCD (liquid crystal display) A display technology that creates images by manipulating light within a layer of liquid crystal.

LED (light emmitting diode) monitor A flat-panel monitor that uses LEDs to provide backlight.

Link To create a connection between source data and the copy in a new file; the copy in the new file is updated every time a change is made to the source data.

Liquid crystal display *See* LCD.

Local area network (LAN) A network in which the computers and peripheral devices are located relatively close to each other, generally in the same building, and are usually connected with cables.

Log in/log on To sign in with a user name and password before being able to use a computer.

Magnetic storage media An object that stores data as magnetized particles on a surface.

Mainframe computer A computer used by larger business and government agencies that provides centralized storage, processing, and management for large amounts of data.

Malware A broad term that describes any program that is intended to cause harm or convey information to others without the owner's permission.

MB *See* megabyte.

Megabyte (MB) 1,048,576 bytes, or about one million bytes.

Megahertz (MHz) One million cycles per second.

Memory A set of storage locations on the main circuit board that store instructions and data.

Memory capacity The amount of data that the device can handle at any given time. *Also called* storage capacity.

MHz *See* megahertz.

Microprocessor A silicon chip, located on the motherboard, that is responsible for executing instructions to process data; *also called* processor or central processing unit (CPU).

Mininotebook computer *See* subnotebook computer.

Modem Stands for modulator-demodulator; a device that converts the digital signals from your computer into analog signals that can traverse ordinary phone lines, and then converts analog signals back into digital signals at the receiving computer.

Monitor The TV-like peripheral device that displays the output from the computer.

Motherboard The main circuit board of the computer on which processing tasks occur.

Mouse A pointing device that has a rolling ball on its underside and two or more buttons for clicking commands; you control the movement of the pointer by moving the entire mouse around on your desk.

MP3 player A hand-held computer that is used primarily to play and store music, but that can also be used to play digital movies or television shows, allow you to listen to FM radio stations, and access the Internet and email.

Multimedia authoring software Software that allows you to record digital sound files, video files, and animations that can be included in presentations and other documents.

Netbook A type of subnotebook computer that is primarily designed to allow isers to access the Internet and check email. *See* also slate tablet computer.

Network Two or more computers that share data and resources and which are connected to each other and to peripheral devices.

Network interface card (NIC) The card in a computer on a network that creates a communications channel between the computer and the network.

Network software Software that establishes the communications protocols that will be observed on the network and controls the "traffic flow" as data travels throughout the network.

NIC *See* network interface card.

Node Any device connected to a network.

Nonvolatile memory *See* read-only memory.

Notebook computer A small, lightweight computer designed for portability. *Also called* laptop computer.

Object linking and embedding (OLE) The ability to use data created in one application in a file created by another application.

OLE *See* object linking and embedding.

Operating environment An operating system that provides a graphical user interface, such as Microsoft Windows and the MAC OS.

Operating system Software that allocates system resources, manages storage space, maintains security, detects equipment failure, and controls basic input and output.

Optical storage device A polycarbonate disk coated with a reflective metal on which data is recorded using laser technology as a trail of tiny pits or dark spots in the surface of the disk; the data that these pits or spots represent can then be "read" with a beam of laser light.

Output The result of the computer processing input.

Output device A device, such as a monitor or printer, that displays output.

Pages per minute (ppm) The unit of measurement for the speed of laser and inkjet printers.

PAN *See* personal area network.

PC *See* personal computer.

Peer-to-peer network A network in which all the computers essentially are equal, and programs and data are distributed among them.

Peripheral device The components of a computer that accomplish its input, output, and storage functions.

Permanent memory *See* read-only memory.

Personal area network (PAN) A network in which two or more devices communicate directly with each other.

Personal computer (PC) A computer typically used by a single user in the home or office for general computing tasks such as word processing, working with photographs or graphics, e-mail, and Internet access.

Pharm To break into a DNS server and redirect any attempts to access a particular Web site to a spoofed site.

Phish To send e-mails to customers or potential customers of a legitimate Web site asking them to click a link in the e-mail and then verify their personal information; the link leads to a spoofed site.

Photo editing software Software that allows you to manipulate digital photos.

Pixel One of the small dots in a matrix into which a graphics display is divided.

Pointer A small arrow or other symbol on the screen controlled by a pointing device.

Pointing device A device, such as a mouse or trackball, that controls the pointer.

Pointing stick A small, eraser-like device embedded among the typing keys on a notebook computer that you push up, left, right, or down to move the pointer; buttons for clicking commands are located in front of the spacebar.

Port *See* expansion port.

ppm *See* pages per minute.

Presentation software Software that allows you to display or project graphics and other information before a group, print them for quick reference, or transmit them to remote computers.

Printer The peripheral computer component that produces a hard copy of the text or graphics processed by the computer.

Process To modify data in a computer.

Processor *See* microprocessor.

Program A list of instructions that the computer uses to perform a specific task.

Programming language Software used to write computer instructions.

Protocol The set of rules that establishes the orderly transfer of data between the sender and the receiver in data communications.

PS/2 port A port through which a keyboard or a mouse is connected.

Quad-core processor A CPU with four processors on the chip.

RAM *See* random access memory.

RAM cache *See* cache memory.

Random access memory (RAM) Chips on cards plugged into the motherboard that temporarily hold programs and data while the computer is turned on. *Also called* volatile memory or temporary memory.

Read-only memory (ROM) A chip on the motherboard that is prerecorded with and permanently stores the set of instructions that the computer uses when you turn it on. *Also called* nonvolatile memory or permanent memory.

Receiver The computer or peripheral at the message's destination in data communications.

Record A collection of data items in a database.

Resolution The number of pixels that a monitor displays.

ROM *See* read-only memory.

Router A device that controls traffic between network components and usually has a built-in firewall.

Scanner A device that transfers the content on a piece of paper into memory; you place a piece of paper on the glass, a beam of light moves across the glass, similar to a photocopier, and stores the image or words on the piece of paper as digital information.

Screen size The diagonal measurement from one corner of the screen to the other.

Scroll wheel A wheel on a mouse that you roll to scroll the page on the screen.

SDRAM *See* synchronous dynamic RAM.

Security The steps a computer owner takes to prevent unauthorized use of or damage to the computer.

Semipermanent memory *See* complementary metal oxide semiconductor memory.

Sender The computer that originates the message in data communications.

Server A computer on a network that acts as the central storage location for programs and provides mass storage for most of the data used on the network.

Single-core processor A CPU with one processor on the chip.

Slate computer A thin computer primarily used to read electronic books, view video, and access the Internet, and that does not have an external keyboard or a mouse; instead users touch the screen or use a stylus to accomplish tasks.

Slot *See* expansion slot.

Smartphone A handheld computer used to make and received phone calles, maintain an address book, electronic appointment book, calculator, and notepad, send email, connect to the Internet, play music, take photos or video, and perform some of the same functions as a PC, such as word processing.

Software The intangible components of a computer system, particularly the programs that the computer needs to perform a specific task.

Solid state storage *See* flash mamory.

Source The file from which data is copied or linked into another file.

Specifications The technical details about a hardware component.

Spell check The feature in document production software that helps you avoid typographical and grammatical errors.

Spoof To create a Web site that looks exactly like another legitimate site on the Web but steals the information people enter.

Spreadsheet software Software that helps you analyze numerical data.

Spyware Software that track a computer user's Internet usage and sends this data back to the company or person that created it, usually without the computer user's permission or knowledge.

Standalone computer A personal computer that is not connected to a network.

Storage capacity *See* memory capacity.

Strong password A string of at least eight characters of upper and lowercase letters and numbers.

Subnotebook computers Notebook computers that are smaller and lighter than ordinary notebooks. *Also called* ultraportable computer and mini notebook.

Supercomputer The largest and fastest type of computer used by large corporations and government agencies for processing a tremendous volume of data.

Synchronous dynamic RAM (SDRAM) RAM that is synchronized with the CPU to allow faster access to its contents.

System resource Any part of the computer system, including memory, storage devices, and the microprocessor, that can be used by a computer program.

System software A collection of programs and data that helps the computer carry out its basic operating tasks.

Tablet PC A computer designed for portability that includes the capability of recognizing ordinary handwriting on the screen.

TB *See* terabyte.

Telecommunications The transmission of data over a comparatively long distance using a phone line.

Temporary memory *See* random access memory.

Terabyte (TB) 1,024 GB, or approximately one trillion bytes.

Toner A powdery substance used by laser printers to transfer a laser image onto paper.

Touch pad A touch-sensitive device on a laptop computer that you drag your finger over to control the pointer; buttons for clicking commands are located in front of the touch pad.

Touchscreen A display that shows you output and allows you to touch it with your finger or a stylus to input commands.

Trackball A pointing device with a rolling ball on the top side and buttons for clicking commands; you control the movement of the pointer by moving the ball.

Ultraportable computer *See* subnotebook computer.

Universal Serial Bus port *See* USB port.

URL An address on the Web.

USB (Universal Serial Bus) port A high-speed port to which you can connect a device with a USB connector to have the computer recognize the device and allow you to use it immediately.

USB connector A small, rectangular plug attached to a peripheral device and that you connect to a USB port.

USB drive *See* USB flash storage drive.

USB flash storage device A popular type of flash memory. *Also called* USB drive or flash drive.

Utility A type of system software that augments the operating system by taking over some of its responsibility for allocating hardware resources.

VGA (video graphics array) port A port that transmits analog video.

Video card *See* graphics card.

Video display adapter *See* graphics card.

Video editing software Software that allows you to edit video by clipping it, adding captions or a soundtrack, or rearranging clips.

Virtual memory Space on the computer's storage devices that simulates additional RAM.

Virus A harmful program that instructs a computer to perform destructive activities, such as erasing a disk drive; variants are called worms and Trojan horses.

Virus protection software *See* antivirus software.

Volatile memory *See* random access memory.

WAN *See* wide area network.

Web *See* World Wide Web.

Web browser *See* browser.

Web site creation and management software Software that allows you to create and manage Web sites and to see what the Web pages will look like as you create them.

Wi-Fi *See* wireless fidelity.

Wide area network (WAN) A network that connects one or more LAN.

WiMAX (Worldwide Interoperability for Microwave Access) A standard of wireless communication defined by the IEEE that allows computers to communicate wirelessly over many miles; signals are transmitted from WiMAX towers to a WiMAX receiver in a device.

Wireless fidelity The term created by the nonprofit Wi-Fi Alliance to describe networks connected using a standard radio frequency established by the Institute of Electrical and Electronics Engineers (IEEE); frequently referred to as Wi-Fi.

Wireless local area network (WLAN) A LAN connected using high frequency radio waves rather than cables.

WLAN *See* wireless local area network.

Word size The amount of data that is processed by a microprocessor at one time.

Worksheet In spreadsheet software, a grid composed of columns and rows that create cells at their intersection; you type data and formulas into cells.

Workstation A computer that is connected to a network.

Worldwide Interoperability for Microwave Access *See* WiMAX.

World Wide Web (Web) A huge database of information that is stored on network servers in places that allow public access.

Index

A

adware, ECC 20
American Standard Code for Information
    Interchange (ASCII), ECC 6, 7
analog signals, ECC 19
anti-spyware software, ECC 20
antivirus software, ECC 20, 21
application software, ECC 24–25
architecture, ECC 4
ASCII (American Standard Code for
    Information Interchange), ECC 6, 7
assistive devices, ECC 12

B

basic input/output system (BIOS), ECC 8
BD-R discs, ECC 11
BD-RE discs, ECC 11
binary digits, ECC 6, 7
BIOS (basic input/output system), ECC 8
bits, ECC 6
bits per second (bps), ECC 19
Blu-ray discs, ECC 10
Bluetooth, ECC 18
boot process, ECC 8
bps (bits per second), ECC 19
broadband connections, ECC 19
browsers, ECC 20
built-in graphics cards, ECC 14
bytes, ECC 6

C

cables, ECC 16
cache memory, ECC 8
cards, ECC 4
CD (compact disc), ECC 10
CD-R (compact disc recordable), ECC 11
CD-RW (compact disc rewritable), ECC 11
central processing unit (CPU), ECC 4, 5
channels, ECC 16
characters per second (cps), ECC 14
circuit boards, ECC 4
circuits, ECC 4
client/server networks, ECC 18
clients, ECC 18
clip art, ECC 24
clock speed, ECC 5
cloud computing, ECC 25
CMOS (complementary metal oxide
    semiconductor) memory, ECC 8
commands, ECC 4
compact disc (CD), ECC 10

compact disc recordable (CD-R), ECC 11
compact disc rewritable (CD-RW), ECC 11
complementary metal oxide semiconductor
    (CMOS) memory, ECC 8
computers
    application software, ECC 24–25
    computer systems, ECC 4–5
    data communications, ECC 16–17
    data representation, ECC 6–7
    input devices, ECC 12–13
    memory, ECC 8–9
    networks, ECC 18–19
    output devices, ECC 14–15
    overview, ECC 1
    security threats, ECC 20–21
    storage media, ECC 10–11
    system software, ECC 22–23
    types of, ECC 2–3
configuration, ECC 4
controller cards, ECC 16
cps (characters per second), ECC 14
CPU cache, ECC 8
CPU (central processing unit), ECC 4, 5

D

data, ECC 4
data bus, ECC 16
data communications, ECC 16–17
data files, ECC 10
data representation, ECC 6–7
database management software, ECC 24
databases, ECC 24
desktop computers, ECC 2
device drivers, ECC 16
devices
    input, ECC 12–13
    output, ECC 14–15
digital signals, ECC 19
digital subscriber line (DSL), ECC 19
digital video interface (DVI) ports, ECC 16, 17
DNS (Domain Name System) server, ECC 20
document production software, ECC 24
dot matrix printers, ECC 14
dot pitch (dp), ECC 14
drivers, ECC 16
DSL (digital subscriber line), ECC 19
dual-core processors, ECC 5
DVD, ECC 10
DVD-R, ECC 11
DVD-RW, ECC 11
DVD+R, ECC 11
DVD+RW, ECC 11
DVI (digital video interface) ports, ECC 16, 17

E

embedding, ECC 24
ergonomic keyboards, ECC 12, 13
Ethernet ports, ECC 16, 17
executable files, ECC 10
expansion cards, ECC 16
expansion ports, ECC 16, 17
expansion slots, ECC 16

F

fields, ECC 24
files, ECC 10
firewalls, ECC 20
FireWire, ECC 16
flash drive, ECC 10, 11
flash memory, ECC 10
flash memory cards, ECC 10
flat panel monitors, ECC 14
fonts, ECC 24

G

gigabyte (GB), ECC 6
gigahertz (GHz), ECC 5
graphics cards, ECC 14
graphics displays, ECC 14
graphics processors, ECC 14
graphics software, ECC 24
GUI (graphical user interface), ECC 22, 23

H

hand-held computers, ECC 2
hard copy, ECC 14
hard disks, ECC 10
hardware, ECC 4
hardware firewalls, ECC 20
HDMI (high-definition multimedia interface)
    ports, ECC 16

I

I/O (input and output), ECC 22
IEEE 1394 interface, ECC 16, 17
information management software, ECC 24
infrared technology, ECC 18
inkjet printers, ECC 14, 15
input, ECC 4
input devices, ECC 4, 12–13
integration, ECC 24

interface cards, ECC 16
Internet, ECC 18